Storytelling Recipes

for Christian Teachers

Bert Minkin
Illustrated by Carolyn Braun

SAINT LOUIS

Scripture quotations are taken from the HOLY BIBLE, NEW INTERNATIONAL VERSION®. NIV®. Copyright © 1973, 1978, 1984 by International Bible Society. Used by permission of Zondervan Publishing House. All rights reserved.

Copyright © 1996 Concordia Publishing House
3558 S. Jefferson Avenue, St. Louis, MO 63118-3968
Manufactured in the United States of America

1 2 3 4 5 6 7 8 9 10   05 04 03 02 01 00 99 98 97 96

Introduction

A recipe is a tool used to achieve a goal. My goal in this book has been to provide you with Christ-centered storytelling resources to help you share God's love with young children.

Good recipes are user-friendly. These recipes can be adapted to your special teaching needs. You can substitute props, adjust the number of dramatic roles to fit the size of your class, and adjust the vocabulary.

These recipes can be used in day, weekday, vacation Bible school, and Sunday school openings and classrooms. They can be used in presenting school chapel services, children's lessons in church, and school and church programs. They can also be used by parents as they share God's love at home.

Display your Bible each time you tell a story. Remind children that the Bible is God's Word—different from all other books, inspired by Him. As you begin, clear the children's desks, tables, or storytelling area so that they will not be distracted. Set the mood by singing a song together or praying. Thank God for the opportunity to teach His lambs and ask His blessing on your teaching.

Share your personal witness with the children. Let them feel God's love in every story you tell. Adjust the length of the story to meet their attention span. All action should take place at their eye level. Your hands and face are storytelling tools that the children need to see. Practice telling the story with appropriate movements, gestures, facial expressions, and vocal tone. Young children are especially attentive to character voices and sound effects.

You will find a wide range of storytelling formats and tools in these recipes—props, echo pantomimes, role-playing, repetition of key words, riddles, questions, drama, and more. Adapt and expand them to fit your children's needs and other stories you wish to teach.

I hope that sharing these Christ-centered storytelling recipes will give you joy in sharing God's love. I will humbly share that joy every time you use them.

Bert Minkin

Creation

Scripture: Genesis 1:1–31

Central Truth: God created you and cares for you. He will help you love and care for His world.

Props: Gift wrap a globe in a large box.

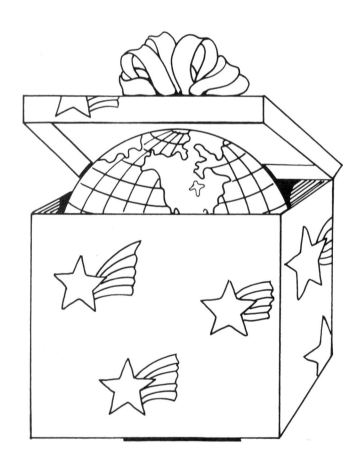

Telling the Story

Display box. Boys and girls, do you like to get gifts? *Let children respond.* Long, long ago, God created a very special gift for us. He created His gift in six days.

First, God created light where there had only been darkness. Then God created the sky and made rivers, lakes, seas, and oceans of water. God created dry land and all kinds of plants to grow on it. The beautiful trees, grass, flowers, and bushes we enjoy were all created by God.

The sun, moon, and stars that shine over us were all a part of God's beautiful creation. Next, God wanted living creatures to enjoy all that He had created. God spoke, and for the very first time, birds flew in the sky. *Have children copy you as you flap your arms.* Fish swam in the water. *Mimic swimming.* Bees buzzed among God's flowers. *Mimic buzzing.* God made *(mimic sounds each animal makes after naming it)* dogs, cows, sheep, and all other kinds of animals.

God created many wonderful things on each of those *(have children count on their fingers with you)* one, two, three, four, five, six days, but He was not finished yet.

On the sixth day, God also made His most beloved creatures to rule over all of His creation. God made people, Adam and Eve, in His image.

Point to box. Boys and girls, do you love to receive gifts? *Let children respond.* When you receive a gift, do you thank the giver? Do you do your very best to take care of the gift? *Let children respond.*

Now let's open our special gift box. *Ask children to help you open the box and hold up the globe.* God loves you and created His world for you.

When you receive a gift, you thank the giver and do your very best to take good care of the gift. Let's thank God for the wonderful gift of His creation and ask Him to help us care for His earth.

God's Promise to Adam and Eve

Scripture: Genesis 2:15–3:24

Central Truth: God loved Adam and Eve, even after they sinned, and promised to send His Son as their Savior and ours.

Props: Write the word **sin** on a small piece of red construction paper for each child. You will also need a box.

Preparation: Quickly rehearse the three children who will play Adam, Eve, and Jesus.

Telling the Story

Boys and girls, today we will learn about the first people that God made. First, God made a man named Adam. *Adam enters.* Then God made a woman named Eve. *Eve enters.* God let Adam and Eve live in the beautiful Garden of Eden, which He made for them. *Adam and Eve smile at their beautiful surroundings.*

Adam: God gives us everything we want to eat and drink.

Eve: We love living in His Garden of Eden.

God told Adam and Eve they could enjoy eating delicious fruit from all but one of His trees. He told them never to eat the fruit from the tree growing in the middle of the garden.

Adam and Eve foolishly listened when the devil tempted them to eat from that tree. They did what they wanted to do instead of listening to God. That was the very first sin. *Adam and Eve hold a red badge of "sin" over their hearts and look around guiltily.*

Adam: We disobeyed God. We're afraid!

Eve: We will hide from God! *Adam and Eve crouch as if they are hiding.*

Of course, God knew where Adam and Eve were. *Adam and Eve slowly rise, keeping their heads bowed and acting ashamed.* God helped Adam and Eve understand that they had sinned when they disobeyed Him. God took away Adam and Eve's privilege of living in the Garden of Eden.

Adam and Eve distribute red badges of sin to everyone in the class. Have the children copy you in holding the badge over their hearts. Since Adam and Eve sinned, all of us are born into sin. I sin *(point to your badge)* and you sin *(point to children's badges).*

But God still loved Adam and Eve, even after they had sinned. God promised that one day He would send His own Son, Jesus, to die on the cross to take away their sin. *Jesus enters, holding empty box.*

Jesus: I am Jesus. I will take away the sins of Adam and Eve. I will take away your sins too. *Jesus goes to each child and collects badges into box.*

God still loved Adam and Eve, even after they had sinned. God will always love you too.

Noah's Ark

Scripture: Genesis 9:1–17

Central Truth: God loves you and will always protect you just as He protected Noah's family and the animals on the ark.

Props: Sheets of red, orange, yellow, green, blue, and purple construction paper

Preparation: Teach children to wiggle their fingers up and down when you say "rain," place their hands over their ears when you say "thunder," and put their hands over their eyes when you say "lightning." Pass out construction paper for children to hold.

Telling the Story

After God made His world, He filled it with people. After a while, the people began to forget about God. God told a man who still loved Him, named Noah, to build a big boat called an ark. God told Noah to take his wife, his three sons and their wives, and two of every kind of animal onto the ark. There were *(have children make each animal's sound after you name the animal)* sheep, cows, dogs, cats, monkeys, horses, and many other kinds of animals and birds.

Then God sent *(lead children in wiggling fingers each time you say "rain")* rain. For 40 days and 40 nights, there was rain, *(cover ears)* thunder, and *(cover eyes)* lightning. The water rose higher and higher and higher until it covered all the land on the whole earth.

But God kept Noah safe. God protected all the people and animals on the ark.

After 40 days and 40 nights, the rain *(wiggle fingers)*, thunder *(cover ears)*, and lightning *(cover eyes)* stopped. Many more days passed before the land was dry and Noah and his family and the animals could come out of the ark. When it was safe, God let Noah know that all the people and animals could live on land again. God promised that He would never again cover the whole earth with water.

God gave Noah a special sign that He would always keep His promise. Noah looked up in the sky and saw *(have children hold up colors as you name them)* red, orange, yellow, green, blue, and purple. Noah saw a rainbow!

Boys and girls, God loved and protected Noah's family and all the animals on the ark. God made all the beautiful colors of the rainbow to remind us of His loving promise. God loves you and will always protect you.

God's Promise to Abram

Scripture: Genesis 15:1–9

Central Truth: God keeps all His promises, including His most precious promise to send Jesus to be our Savior.

Props: A picture of a star-filled sky (or cover a sheet of black or dark blue construction paper with gummed stars) and a watch

Preparation: Quickly rehearse the child who will play Abram.

Telling the Story

Hold up picture of starry sky. Boys and girls, have you ever looked up in the nighttime sky and seen all the stars? *Let children respond.* God made more shining stars in the sky than you could possibly count.

Long ago, God told Abram to go out at night and look at the stars in the sky. God loved Abram and had led him to a new home in the beautiful land of Canaan. God promised that the new land would always belong to Abram and his family.

Abram and his wife, Sarai, had no children. *Abram looks sad and bows his head and folds his hands to pray.* He prayed that God would help him and his wife have a child.

God told Abram to try to count all the stars in the sky. *Abram looks up and frantically tries to count the stars on his fingers, then gives up.*

Abram: Lord, there are more stars than I could ever count!

Then God promised that one day Abram would have more children than he could count. And one day, Jesus would be born from Abram's family to die on the cross for us and be our Savior from sin.

Abram looks at his watch. Time went by. But God kept His promise. Even though Abram and Sarai were very old, Sarai had a little boy. They named him Isaac. Isaac and his wife would have children, and their children would have children, and many more children would be descended from Abram, until finally Jesus would be born.

God kept His promises to Abram. He even gave Abram a new name. *Hold up star picture.* There were many more stars than Abram could count. God would give Abram many more descendants than he could count. God's new name for Abram was Abraham. Abraham means "father of many."

God loved Abraham and kept His promises. God loves you and keeps all His promises to you too.

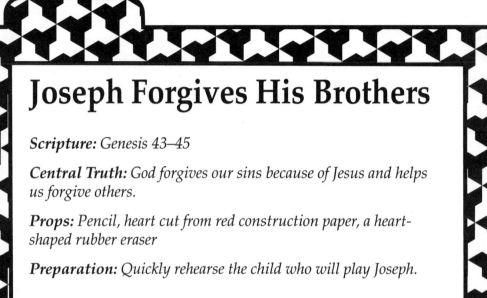

Joseph Forgives His Brothers

Scripture: Genesis 43–45

Central Truth: God forgives our sins because of Jesus and helps us forgive others.

Props: Pencil, heart cut from red construction paper, a heart-shaped rubber eraser

Preparation: Quickly rehearse the child who will play Joseph.

Telling the Story

Boys and girls, today we will learn how Joseph shared God's love with his 11 brothers. God blessed Joseph with great *(point to your head)* wisdom and a loving *(point to your heart)* heart. Even when Joseph was a child, his wisdom amazed his father, Jacob, and his brothers. Joseph told them about the wonderful dreams God gave him.

Jacob loved all of his sons, but he was especially fond of Joseph. One day, he gave Joseph a beautiful new coat to wear. This hurt the brothers' feelings and made them jealous. *Use the pencil to draw a frown on the paper heart.* Pencils make marks on paper. But the brothers' jealousy made a mark on their hearts. They foolishly thought they could take away that hurt by doing something mean to Joseph.

The brothers sold Joseph to some slave traders who carried him away to Egypt. They told their father that Joseph had been killed by a wild animal. But doing that mean thing and telling that lie did not take the hurt away.

God took care of Joseph in Egypt. He showed Joseph how to use his wisdom to teach the Egyptian people how to save food in big barns. They would eat that food during seven years when God did not send rain and food stopped growing in Egypt. Joseph's plan worked so well that Egypt even had enough food to sell to its neighbors. The king rewarded Joseph by making him a ruler and letting him decide who could have extra food.

One day, Joseph's brothers came to Egypt, hoping to buy some food to take home to Jacob. Joseph recognized his brothers, but they did not know him. They had no idea that he had become a powerful ruler in Egypt.

Do you think that Joseph's heart was hurt by the mean things his brothers had done? *Let children respond.* Do you think that Joseph tried to hurt his brothers to get even? *Let children respond.*

God gave Joseph wisdom and filled his heart with love. Watch what Joseph did. *Point to the frown on the heart. Joseph erases the frown with the heart-shaped eraser.*

Joseph: I will forgive my brothers. I will share God's love with them.

Joseph gave his brothers plenty of food and invited them to live in Egypt. *Hold up pencil and eraser.* An eraser takes away pencil marks from paper. *Place your hand over your heart.* Sharing God's love and forgiveness took away the hurt from Joseph's heart.

God forgives our sins because Jesus suffered and died in our place. Joseph shared God's love by forgiving his brothers. You can share God's love and forgiveness by forgiving others too.

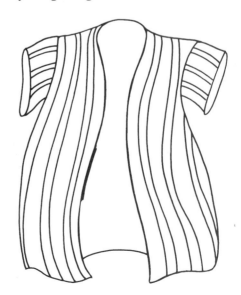

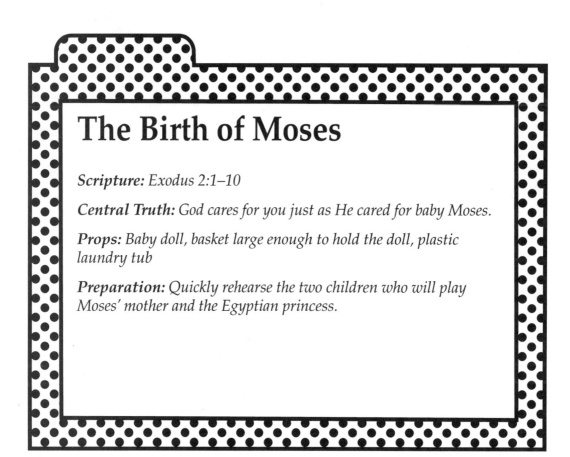

The Birth of Moses

Scripture: Exodus 2:1–10

Central Truth: God cares for you just as He cared for baby Moses.

Props: Baby doll, basket large enough to hold the doll, plastic laundry tub

Preparation: Quickly rehearse the two children who will play Moses' mother and the Egyptian princess.

Telling the Story

Boys and girls, have any of you ever helped take care of a baby? *Let children respond.* In this story, I'm going to play the part of Miriam. She took care of her baby brother in a special way.

Hello, my name is Miriam. I lived in Egypt a long time ago. The Egyptian king was very mean to my people. My mother was afraid he would take my baby brother away. To hide him from the bad king, Mother covered a basket with tar so it could float in the water. Then she put my brother into the basket. *Mother prepares basket and places doll inside.*

Walk with mother to put basket in tub. Mother and I took my brother to the Nile River and put his basket in the water. *Kneel and fold hands.* We asked God to take care of my brother and see that nothing bad happened to him.

Crouch down as if hiding and keeping an eye on basket. Mother told me to stay by the river and watch. *Princess walks to tub and peers in basket.* A beautiful young woman came to the river to take a bath. It was the mean king's daughter! The princess noticed my brother's basket and asked her maid to see what it was.

Princess picks up doll. The princess gently picked up my brother and told him not to cry. I could see she was very kind. *Jump up and run to princess.* I jumped up and asked the princess if she would like a kind woman to nurse the baby and take care of him.

Princess: Wonderful! Please bring her to me.

Lead mother to princess.

Mother: I'm very good with children. I'll help you take care of this baby.

My mother helped the kind princess take care of my brother. Mother taught my brother about God and how much He loves us. You know my brother by the special name the princess gave him—Moses.

God took care of my baby brother Moses. When Moses grew up, God helped him lead my people away from the mean king. God kept baby Moses safe. God loves and protects you too.

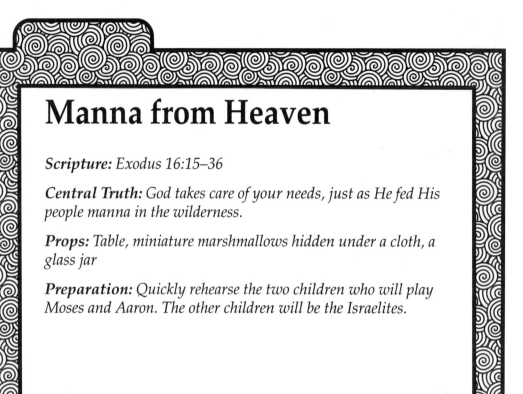

Manna from Heaven

Scripture: Exodus 16:15–36

Central Truth: God takes care of your needs, just as He fed His people manna in the wilderness.

Props: Table, miniature marshmallows hidden under a cloth, a glass jar

Preparation: Quickly rehearse the two children who will play Moses and Aaron. The other children will be the Israelites.

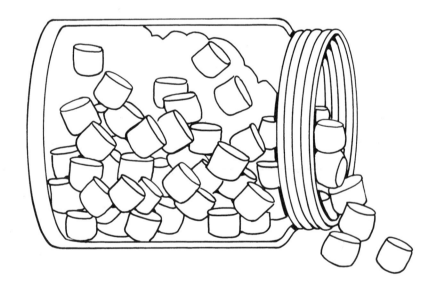

Telling the Story

Boys and girls, today we will learn how God took care of His children after He led them out of Egypt. They spent the next 40 years wandering in the hot, dry desert. Everywhere they looked was covered with sand. There was no food to eat. God's people grew worried.

Israelites: What will we eat?

God told Moses what to tell them.

Moses: God loves you and will take care of you. Just follow His instructions.

The next morning, the ground was covered with a wonderful food that no one had seen before. *Remove the cloth and reveal marshmallows.*

Moses told the people what God wanted them to do. God would give them enough manna for one day at a time. It would get rotten and smelly if they tried to keep it overnight. God would give them manna to gather every morning for *(have children count with you)* one, two, three, four, five, six days a week.

On the sixth day, God had Moses tell the people to collect a double portion of manna. They could eat all they needed on the sixth day and save their leftovers for the seventh day. God promised that this leftover manna would not spoil.

On the seventh day of the week, *(cover marshmallows)* God's children found no manna on the ground. God wanted them to use the seventh day to praise and thank Him and to rest. This day of the week was called the Sabbath.

God had Moses tell his brother, Aaron, something special to do. *Moses uncovers marshmallows and hands jar to Aaron.*

Moses: Aaron, fill this jar with manna. We will keep it in a special place forever. God wants us to remember that He always takes care of us.

Aaron fills the jar and reverently sets it on the table.

God fed His children with manna for 40 years in the desert. God always loves you and takes care of your needs. He even sent His own Son—the Bread of Life—to die on the cross for you and win you eternal life in heaven.

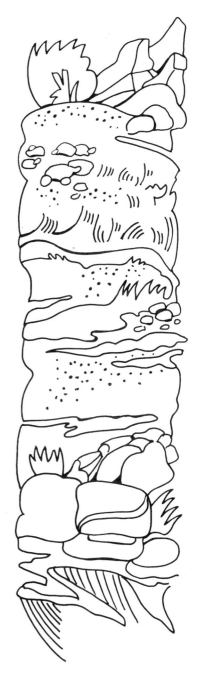

God Gives His Ten Commandments

Scripture: Exodus 20:1–21

Central Truth: God gave us His Ten Commandments to help us love Him and share His love with others.

Props: A large mirror, a comb, a washcloth

Preparation: Stand beside the mirror as you tell the story.

Telling the Story

Boys and girls, when do you look at yourself in a mirror? *Let children respond.* Mirrors help us see in many ways. Mirrors in cars help drivers see the other cars around them. At home, mirrors help you brush your teeth, comb your hair, and get dressed properly. Mirrors help you see exactly how you look and help you correct your mistakes.

When I want to see if my hair needs combing, I look at my reflection in a mirror. *Look in mirror and comb hair.* Now the mirror is helping me see how to comb my hair properly.

A long time ago, God told Moses to climb to the top of Mount Sinai. That's where God gave Moses His Ten Commandments. Moses shared the commandments with God's people.

The Ten Commandments are God's special rules for showing us how to love Him and one another. They remind us to put God first and treat each other respectfully.

Do you have rules to obey at home? *Let children respond.* God's Ten Commandments are the most special rules of all. *Point to the mirror.* Mirrors help us see how we look. God's Ten Commandments are like a special mirror telling us how we're living.

What do you do when you look in the mirror and see that your face is dirty? *Let children respond.* That's right. *Hold up the washcloth.* You wash your face.

When we look at the Ten Commandments, we can see that our lives aren't perfectly clean. We might say God's name in a bad way. We might tease our friend, or hit our sister, or talk back to Mom or Dad. Then we know that we can't keep God's commandments perfectly by ourselves. We ask Jesus to forgive us and help us share His love.

God loved His children in the Old Testament times and gave them His Ten Commandments to help them live His way. God loves us too. He sent His own Son, Jesus, to live on earth and keep the commandments perfectly for us. God will help us remember His commandments and share His love.

David and Goliath

Scripture: 1 Samuel 17

Central Truth: *God loves you and will always help you, just as He helped David.*

Preparation: *Practice reciting the echo pantomime and making the motions. Ask the children to echo your words and mimic your actions.*

Telling the Story

Goliath was big.
> *Reach high in the air.*

Goliath was mean.
> *Shake fists and scowl.*

He was a big, mean
> *Reach high and scowl.*

Philistine.
> *Place hands on hips and scowl.*

David was small,
> *Stretch one hand down toward floor.*

Gentle and small.
> *Gently smile and stretch one hand down toward floor.*

He was a child
> *Pretend to rock baby in arms.*

Of God.
> *Point up.*

God made David
> *Stretch one hand down toward floor.*

Very powerful.
> *Flex muscles.*

God made Goliath
> *Reach high in air.*

Fall very low.
> *Squat down.*

All was well.
> *Smile broadly.*

Goliath fell
> *Look down at floor.*

To the powerful God
> *Point up.*

Of Israel.
> *Fold hands in prayer.*

Boys and girls, David knew that God would protect him from Goliath. God loves you, just as He loved David. He will always keep you safe.

Elijah and the Widow

Scripture: 1 Kings 17:7–24

Central Truth: God will always care for your needs, just as He cared for Elijah, the widow, and her son.

Props: A small plastic jar and a small plastic jug

Preparation: Quickly rehearse the three children who will play the roles of Elijah, the widow, and her son.

Telling the Story

Boys and girls, today we will learn how God cared for His helper Elijah, a poor widow, and her only son. Elijah was a prophet. He told people about God's love and about what God wanted them to do. Elijah knew that God would always take care of him.

One day, God told Elijah to go to a little town with a big name—Zarephath. God had told a woman who lived there to take care of Elijah. *Elijah walks over to widow and son.*

Elijah: God has told me that you will feed me. I need to stay strong and healthy to share God's Word.

Widow *(looking worried):* I am just a poor woman with no husband! I have only *(holds up jar)* one jar of flour and *(holds up jug)* one jug of oil. My young son has to eat too. How can I feed the three of us with so little food?

Elijah: God has promised that your jar of flour and jug of oil will be enough. God will take care of us. We will have plenty of food.

Widow: I will do as God says.

All that Elijah said was true. God made that flour and oil last a very long time. The widow used it to make lots of good bread for the three of them to eat. *Elijah, the widow, and her son smile and rub their stomachs.*

God loved Elijah, the widow, and her son, and always gave them what they needed. God loves you and will always give you what you need too.

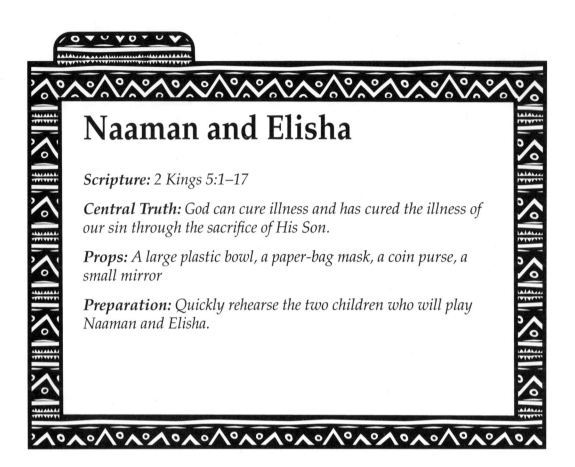

Naaman and Elisha

Scripture: 2 Kings 5:1–17

Central Truth: God can cure illness and has cured the illness of our sin through the sacrifice of His Son.

Props: A large plastic bowl, a paper-bag mask, a coin purse, a small mirror

Preparation: Quickly rehearse the two children who will play Naaman and Elisha.

24

Telling the Story

Boys and girls, today we will learn how God worked through His prophet Elisha to make a man named Naaman well. *Naaman steps forward, wearing paper-bag mask.* Naaman was a rich and powerful leader of a large army of soldiers.

Naaman had a sickness called leprosy that made horrible sores on his skin. All his money and soldiers could not help him get well. The wisest doctors in his country of Syria could not help him either. *Naaman hangs his head sadly.*

Then a little girl told Naaman's wife about a wise man named Elisha who lived in Israel. Elisha was God's prophet. He shared God's Word with His people.

Naaman (*holding up coin purse*): I will go to Israel and find Elisha. I will pay him anything he wants to make me well!

Naaman went to Elisha's house. Elisha sent a messenger to tell Naaman how to get well. Naaman was not at all happy with Elisha's instructions.

Naaman (*stomping his feet angrily*): Elisha says that I should wash myself in the water of the River Jordan seven times. How will that make me well? It sounds too easy!

Naaman had traveled all the way to Israel, and Elisha didn't even bother to talk to him. He sent his servant with the message. None of the doctors in Syria could make Naaman well, and now he is supposed to dunk himself in a muddy river. Boys and girls, should Naaman follow Elisha's instructions? *Let the children respond.* I'm happy to say that Naaman followed Elisha's directions.

Naaman: I will wash myself seven times in the River Jordan. (*Have children count as Naaman dips his hands in bowl seven times. Then Naaman removes mask and looks in mirror.*) I am well! (*Holding up coin purse*) I will reward Elisha for making me well.

Naaman rushed over to pay Elisha. He would give Elisha anything he wanted for making him well. How much money do you think Elisha asked for? *Let children respond.* Boys and girls, Elisha would not let Naaman give him anything at all!

Elisha (*speaking to Naaman*): Naaman, I will not take your money. I did not make you well, God did.

Naaman: I will always thank God and follow His ways.

God washed Naaman clean of the sickness of leprosy. Boys and girls, we have a sickness too, the sickness of sin. God let His Son, Jesus, give His life on the cross so that He could wash us clean of our sin in our Baptism. We thank God with Naaman for making us well.

The Fiery Furnace

Scripture: Daniel 3:1–30

Central Truth: God loves you and protects you, just as He protected the men in the fiery furnace.

Prop: A paper fan

Preparation: Quickly rehearse the seven children who will play the roles of Shadrach, Meshach, Abednego, three soldiers, and the angel.

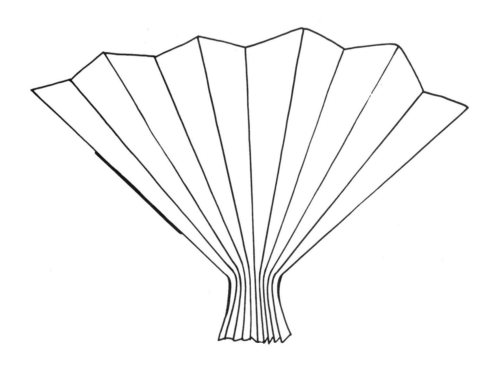

Telling the Story

Boys and girls, in this story, I'll play the role of a king who learned about God's love from three young men named Shadrach, Meshach, and Abednego.

Hello! I am King Nebuchadnezzar. I ruled the land of Babylon a long time ago. One day, I had my workers build a huge golden statue. It was *(stretch arms wide)* 90 feet wide and *(look up and raise arms)* 90 feet tall. I commanded all my people to *(point to children and speak in a stern, commanding voice)* bow down and worship that great big golden statue.

Everyone obeyed my command except three young men who had come from the land of Judah. Their names were Shadrach, Meshach, and Abednego.

Shadrach, Meshach, Abednego: King Nebuchadnezzar, we will not bow down to worship your great big golden statue. We love God. We will only bow down to worship Him.

I got very angry and had my strongest soldiers throw them in a red hot fiery furnace!

Three soldiers *(grabbing Shadrach, Meshach, Abednego and pushing them forward)*: Get into the fiery furnace! We'll stand guard outside the door and see that you never get out.

I wanted to see if God could protect them from red hot fire. I made the fire seven times hotter than it had ever been. The fire was so hot that it killed the soldiers standing outside.

Three soldiers *(gasping for breath)*: We're burning up! We can't stand this fire anymore! *They collapse on the floor.*

Then I looked through the door of the fiery furnace and saw a miracle! *Open eyes wide in amazement as the angel enters and fans Shadrach, Meshach, and Abednego, who bow their heads and fold their hands to pray.*

I saw three men go into the furnace. But when I looked through the door, I saw *(count on your fingers)* one, two, three, *four.* God had sent His angel to protect Shadrach, Meshach, and Abednego, and the angel looked like God's Son!

I called Shadrach, Meshach, and Abednego to come out of the fiery furnace. *Welcome them with open arms and look at them in awe.* God had kept them safe and cool in the fire. I saw how powerful God is.

Boys and girls, God loved Shadrach, Meshach, and Abednego. He protected them and helped them be strong in their faith. God will protect you and keep your faith in Him strong too.

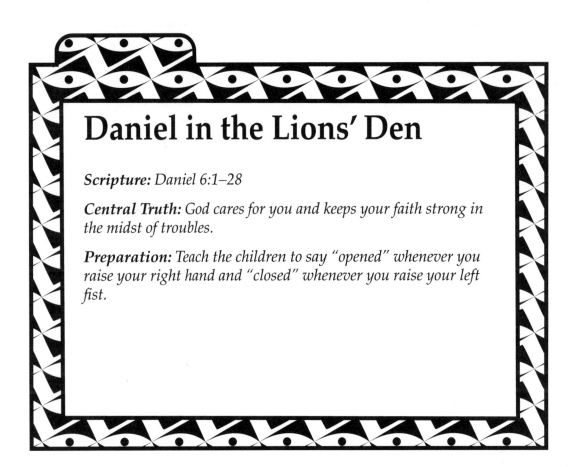

Daniel in the Lions' Den

Scripture: Daniel 6:1–28

Central Truth: *God cares for you and keeps your faith strong in the midst of troubles.*

Preparation: *Teach the children to say "opened" whenever you raise your right hand and "closed" whenever you raise your left fist.*

Telling the Story

Daniel had to leave his home in Judah and live in Babylon long ago. Daniel prayed to God three times every day. He knew that God loved Him and would be with him, even though he was far from home.

The king of Babylon saw that Daniel was a good worker. He let Daniel help him rule the land. Some of the king's other helpers grew jealous. Daniel's heart was *(raise right hand)* opened to God, but the jealous men's hearts were *(raise left fist)* closed to Him. They *(raise right hand)* opened their mouths and said mean things about Daniel. When Daniel refused to pray to the king, they told the king to throw Daniel in a den of lions.

The king had to throw Daniel into a den of big, hungry lions. He *(raise left fist)* closed the den with a big stone. Daniel was left alone with those lions.

But Daniel wasn't really alone. Daniel prayed to God. God *(raise right hand)* opened Daniel's heart. Daniel knew that God would keep him safe. God sent an angel who *(raise left fist)* closed the lions' jaws. They never *(raise right hand)* opened their mouths to eat Daniel.

In the morning, the king rushed to the den and saw that God had kept Daniel safe. The king had the jealous men thrown into the den. When the stone *(raise left fist)* closed the den, the hungry lions' jaws *(raise right hand)* opened wide.

The king saw that God had *(raise left fist)* closed the lions' jaws and kept them from harming Daniel. That's how God *(raise right hand)* opened the king's heart to trust in Him.

God sends His angels to protect you everywhere you go, just as He protected Daniel.

Jonah and the Big Fish

Scripture: Jonah 1–4

Central Truth: God works through us to share the news of His risen Son.

Props: A chair, a pair of earmuffs

Preparation: Quickly rehearse the child who will play the role of Jonah.

Telling the Story

Boys and girls, today we will learn about a man named Jonah who lived long ago in Israel. God told Jonah to go and tell the people of Nineveh about Him. But Jonah was very foolish. He did not want to listen to God.

Jonah: I'm not going to listen to God! I'm going to run away and hide from Him! *Jonah puts on earmuffs and runs in place.*

Silly Jonah! He ran to a boat. The boat started sailing on the sea. There was Jonah, trying to run away and hide from God.

God saw Jonah. He had a big fish come along and swallow Jonah. Now Jonah had to stop running. God had Jonah take a time out. *Jonah stops running and sits on chair.*

Boys and girls, have any of you ever had to take a time out? *Let children respond.* A time out helps us listen and learn. God had Jonah take a time out for three days inside that big fish. Jonah remembered God's great love. He told God he was sorry and that he promised to obey Him.

Jonah *(removing earmuffs and smiling):* I will always listen to God and share His love. I will never try to run and hide again.

God knew that Jonah had listened and learned. God had that big fish spit Jonah out. Jonah's time out was all done. *Jonah stands up and smiles.*

Jonah listened to God. He went to Nineveh and told the people to say that they were sorry for their sins and to turn back to God.

Years later, God sent His own Son, Jesus, to the earth. Jesus died on the cross and stayed in the tomb for three days, just like Jonah stayed in the belly of the fish for three days. Then Jesus came out of the tomb, alive again. God will help us be in the right place at the right time to help us share about Jesus and His love, just as He helped Jonah.

The Shepherds and Angels

Scripture: Luke 2:8–20

Central Truth: God sent His own Son, Jesus, to save us. He will help us share this Good News, just like the shepherds did.

Preparation: Practice reciting the echo pantomime and making the motions. Ask the children to echo your words and mimic your actions.

Telling the Story

God's angel told
Raise arms straight up.
The shepherds in the field,
Shield eyes as if startled.
"Do not be afraid.
Shake your head.
I bring you good news.
Smile broadly.
On this night
Hold up one finger.
In Bethlehem,
Point in distance.
Jesus Christ is born.
Rock a baby in your arms.
Peace on earth
Hold finger to lips.
For everyone.
Hold arms out at sides as if embracing
everyone.
Glory to God
Point up.
In the highest."
Raise both arms.

On that holy night
Fold hands.
In Bethlehem,
Point in distance.
The shepherds saw
Point to eyes.
That Jesus Christ was born.
Rock baby in your arms.

The shepherds told
Point to mouth.
Everyone,
Hold arms out at sides as if embracing
everyone.

"Jesus Christ is born!
Rock baby in your arms.
Glory to God
Point up.
In the highest!"
Raise both arms.

Boys and girls, God sent His own Son, Jesus, to earth so He could grow up to die on the cross in our place. Because of Jesus, our sins are forgiven and we will get to live in heaven. God will help us tell our friends that Good News, just as He helped the shepherds tell the people in Bethlehem.

The Star of Bethlehem

Scripture: Matthew 2:1–12

Central Truth: *God sent His Son to be the Savior of all people. He leads us through His Spirit's guiding.*

Props: *Cut out a yellow construction-paper star and tape it to a short stick or pole. You will need a baby doll and a cradle or a small doll bed (or use a box as a doll bed).*

Preparation: *Place the doll in the cradle some distance from the spot where you will begin the story.*

34

Telling the Story

Boys and girls, today we will learn how God led the Wise Men to find Jesus. Follow me and repeat the words that I say. *Carry the star as the children march behind you. Encourage them to repeat each phrase after you.*

> God's shining star
> Led the Wise Men
> To the town
> Of Bethlehem.
>
> God led them
> Very far to see
> His only Son
> Born for you and me.
>
> The Wise Men saw
> Their newborn King
> On the day we call
> Epiphany.

Gather the children around the cradle. God placed His shining star in the sky to lead the Wise Men to find His Son. By this time, Jesus was a little older, and Mary and Joseph had moved into a house in Bethlehem. God's star led the Wise Men on a long journey, right to the house where Jesus was staying.

God leads us on our journey to heaven too. His Word shines like a star to light our way to heaven.

Jesus Calms the Storm

Scripture: Mark 4:35–41

Central Truth: Jesus cares for us wherever we go, just as He cared for His disciples.

Props: A pillow and a child's sleeping mat or a small cot

Preparation: Quickly rehearse the child who will play the role of Jesus, the two children who will make the sound effects for wind and splashing waves, and the rest of the class, which will be the disciples.

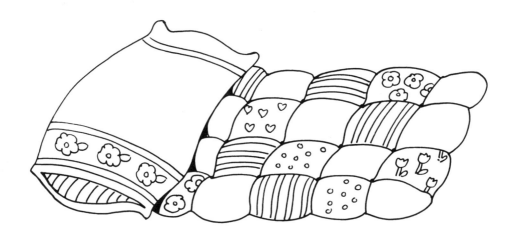

Telling the Story

Have any of you ever taken a boat ride before? *Let children respond.* Today we will learn about a special boat trip that Jesus took with His disciples.

After a busy day, Jesus and His disciples went across a big lake in a boat. Suddenly a great big storm began. Have any of you ever been frightened by a big storm? *Let children respond.*

The disciples were terribly afraid of that storm. The wind blew loud and strong.

Wind: Whoosh! Whoosh! Whoosh!

The waves grew higher and higher and splashed into the boat.

Waves: Splash! Splash! Splash!

The disciples were afraid that the wind and the waves would sink their boat. *Jesus sleeps peacefully on the mat and pillow.* But Jesus slept peacefully at the back of the boat. He wasn't the least bit afraid. The terrified disciples cried out to Jesus:

Disciples: Jesus, please save us from this storm!

The wind and waves resume their sound effects. Jesus gets up, looks at the wind and the waves, and calmly commands:

Jesus: Peace! Be still!

The wind and waves stop immediately. The wind and the waves obeyed Jesus. Now the lake was peaceful and calm, as if there had never been a storm.

Jesus: Why were you so afraid? Didn't you know that I would help you?

Disciples: Who is this? Even the winds and waves obey Him!

Boys and girls, Jesus is the Son of God. He calmed that scary storm to show the disciples, and us, that He can always take care of us. Jesus loved His disciples and took care of them wherever they went. Jesus loves you and takes care of you wherever you go.

Jesus Walks on the Water

Scripture: Matthew 14:22–36

Central Truth: *Jesus helps us keep our eyes on Him as He leads us through every struggle.*

Prop: *Mat or rug large enough for 13 children to sit on*

Preparation: *Quickly rehearse the two children who will play Jesus and Peter and the 11 children who will play the rest of His disciples. Have Peter and the disciples sit on the rug.*

Telling the Story

One night Jesus' disciples were sailing in a boat on a big lake. Have any of you ever taken a boat ride at night? *Let children respond.*

The weather was very windy and the waves grew very high! *Disciples rock back and forth and act frightened.* Suddenly, the disciples saw someone walking towards them. Someone was actually walking on the water! *Jesus starts walking toward mat.* The disciples had never seen anyone who could walk on water. They were very scared. They cried out:

Disciples: It's a ghost!

But the disciples weren't looking at a ghost. Jesus was walking to them on the water!

Jesus: It is Jesus! Don't be afraid.

Then Peter called out:

Peter: Lord, if it's You, tell me to come to You on the water.

Jesus: Come.

Peter got out of the boat and started walking toward Jesus. *Peter gets up from the rug and takes a few bold steps toward Jesus. Then he looks at the water and becomes frightened as he starts to sink.*

Peter: Lord, save me!

Jesus *(reaching out to hold Peter up)*: Don't worry. I will always keep you safe.

Jesus helps Peter into the boat, and they sit down. The disciples stop rocking back and forth to signify the lake has calmed. They look at Jesus, amazed.

Disciples: Truly, Jesus is the Son of God.

Boys and girls, Jesus reached out to Peter and kept him from sinking in that lake. Jesus is always with us. When we are worried and afraid, He promises to help us.

Mary and Martha

Scripture: Luke 10:38–42

Central Truth: God has given us the gift of His Word as our greatest treasure.

Props: Chair, two pillows, and one pair of earmuffs

Preparation: Quickly rehearse the three children who will play the roles of Jesus, Mary, and Martha. As you begin, Jesus sits on the chair, Mary sits on a pillow at his feet, and Martha stands to one side.

Telling the Story

Boys and girls, today we will learn how Jesus shared His love with two friends named Mary and Martha. These two sisters lived in a village called Bethany. They loved having Jesus visit them in their home.

Martha puts on earmuffs and pretends to clean and cook busily. Martha worked hard to get things ready for Jesus. Jesus was a special guest, and she wanted Him to feel comfortable in her home.

Martha: I'm so busy! I have so much work to do, and I have to do it all by myself. Mary is not helping me.

Jesus pantomimes speaking as Mary listens. Martha puts hands on hips and glares at Mary. Then she looks at Jesus.

Martha (*impatiently*): Lord, Mary isn't helping me do my work. She's too busy listening to Your Word. Won't you tell her to help me?

Jesus (*standing and removing earmuffs from Martha's ears*): Martha, I know that you and Mary both want to show your love for Me. You think you can only do that by working hard. But Mary knows what a great gift it is to listen to God's Word. She is learning about My love, and that will never be taken away from her.

Martha sits on second pillow. Both Mary and Martha listen intently as Jesus pantomimes speaking.

Boys and girls, Jesus taught Martha and Mary an important lesson. It is fine to work hard, but it is most important to make time first to learn God's Word. In God's Word, we learn that Jesus loved us enough to die for us. Jesus will help us stay close and listen to Him.

Jesus Blesses the Children

Scripture: Mark 10:13–16

Central Truth: Jesus loves you and will help you trust in Him with childlike faith.

Props: A crepe-paper streamer or length of ribbon and masking tape

Preparation: Stretch a streamer or ribbon across a doorway so that an adult would have to stoop down to walk underneath it. Quickly rehearse the child who will play the role of Jesus. Put him just outside the door.

Telling the Story

Boys and girls, Jesus loves people of all ages. He wants everyone to believe in Him and live in heaven with Him.

One day, some mothers brought their little children to see Jesus. They wanted Jesus to bless their children. Jesus' disciples thought He was too busy to bother with children. They did something very foolish. They tried to stop those mothers from bringing their little children to Jesus.

When Jesus saw how foolishly His disciples were behaving He said:

Jesus: Let the little children come to Me. All people should believe in Me, just as these children do. Little people and big people are all God's children.

Then all the children came to see Jesus. *Lead the children under the ribbon to see Jesus.*

Jesus: Bless you, My little children.

Boys and girls, Jesus shared His love with every one of those children. He said all of us should believe in Him with as much trust as little children do. Jesus loves all people and wants us to live in heaven with Him.

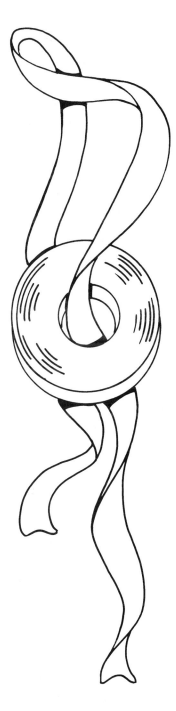

The Parable of the Lost Son

Scripture: Luke 15:11–32

Central Truth: God forgives us, because of Jesus, when sin separates us from Him.

Props: A box with a sign that says: **Lost and Found**; a pair of gloves; several coins. Place all items on a table or desk.

Preparation: Put on the gloves as you begin. Place coins in your pockets.

Telling the Story

Boys and girls, Jesus told this story to teach us how our loving Father forgives us. Once there was a father who had two sons. *Hold up gloved hands.* He loved them both.

Hold up left hand. One day the youngest son asked his father to give him the money that he would inherit when his father died. *Hold up both hands.* So the father gave both sons their share of his money. *Reach into your pockets. Pull out equal amounts of coins and show them to the children.*

Hold up right hand. The older son stayed home and spent his money wisely. *Drop one coin from your right hand on the table and continue to hold the rest.*

Hold up left hand. The other son did just the opposite. He went far away from home and foolishly wasted all his money. *Drop all the coins in your left hand onto the table.* Back at home, the loving father feared that he had lost his youngest son forever. *Look sad as you remove the left glove and drop it into the box.*

But living far away from home with no money taught the young man a lesson. He decided that he would ask his father to forgive him. *Put left glove on again and smile happily.* The lost son went back home, and his father welcomed him gladly. "We're going to have a party!" he announced.

That didn't make the other son happy. *Clench and shake right fist.* He didn't think his father should forgive his brother and celebrate his homecoming. After all, he was the one who had obeyed his father and saved his money, but no one had a celebration for him.

Then the father helped his sons learn something about sharing love. He did not love his lost son *(hold up left hand)* more than the son *(hold up right hand)* who had stayed at home. He was glad to share all that he had with his older son *(hold up right hand)*, but his younger son *(hold up left hand)* had asked for forgiveness and returned home—that was something to celebrate. *Join hands together.*

Hold up box. Boys and girls, do you have a lost-and-found box at school? Have you ever found a lost glove or something else of yours in it? Think how happy you are when you find something that was lost.

Jesus explained that our sin separates us from God, just like the young son who went far away from his father. He wants us to understand that we are sinners who cannot do good things on our own. Yet, God joyfully forgives us because of Jesus and celebrates with His angels when we tell Him we are sorry. God loves you and is happy to keep you close to Him. *Smile and clasp hands together.*

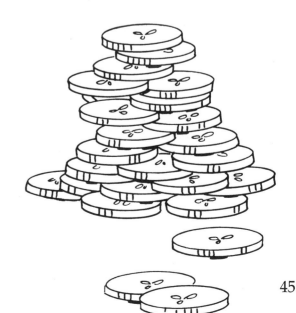

45

The Pharisee and the Tax Collector

Scripture: Luke 18:9–14

Central Truth: God freely forgives us for Jesus' sake when we humbly confess our sins to Him.

Props: Cut three hearts from red construction paper. Draw a smiling face on one and a frowning face on the other two.

Preparation: Quickly rehearse the two children who will play the roles of the Pharisee and the tax collector. Both wear frowning hearts as you begin.

Telling the Story

One day, Jesus told this story about two men. One man was a Pharisee. He thought he was better than other people. He thought that he had never done anything wrong. The other man was a tax collector. This man knew that he had done many things that were wrong.

Both men went to the temple to pray. The Pharisee looked up to heaven and said:

Pharisee: God, thank You for making me better than other people! I'm so happy that I'm not a sinner like that tax collector. I've never done anything wrong!

The tax collector looked deep in his heart and humbly said:

Tax collector: God, I have sinned. Please forgive me.

Boys and girls, God knew that both men had sinned. The Pharisee couldn't see his sins. He never looked into his heart and asked God to forgive him.

The tax collector knew that he did many things that were wrong. He looked deep into his heart and prayed to God for forgiveness. God forgave the sins of one of those men. Which man did God forgive? *Let children respond.*

Yes, God forgave the man who looked deep in his heart and prayed for forgiveness. God forgave the tax collector. *Tax collector removes frowning heart and puts on smiling heart.*

Jesus told this parable to help us learn about God's love for us. By ourselves, we cannot do good things and earn God's love and forgiveness. When we humbly tell God we are sorry for our sins, He gladly forgives us for Jesus' sake.

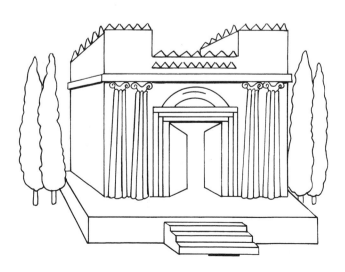

The Parable of the Good Samaritan

Scripture: Luke 10:25–37

Central Truth: Jesus will help us share His love with all people who need it.

Props: A mat, an adhesive bandage, and a chair

Preparation: Quickly rehearse the three children who will play the roles of the Good Samaritan, the priest, and the Levite.

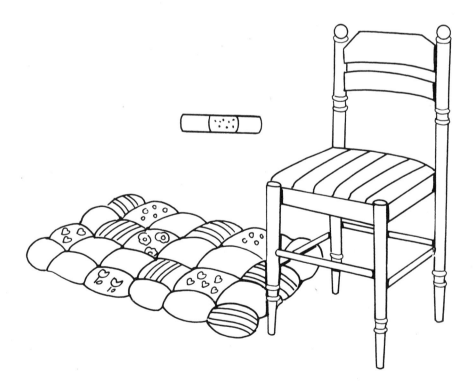

Telling the Story

Boys and girls, let me tell you a story Jesus told about a man who went on a trip long ago.

Hello, I am the traveler in Jesus' story. One day, I was walking down the road from Jerusalem to Jericho. *Start walking, then look frightened and raise your hands in front of your face.* Suddenly, some mean men jumped on me. They hit me very hard and took all of my money. *Grimace in pain and collapse onto the mat on the floor.*

The bad men left me lying there on the ground. I was hurt too badly to move. If only someone would come and help me. *Priest walks over and glances at you, then walks away.*

Priest: I don't have time to stop and help you. I have to get to church.

I kept lying there, hoping someone would take the time to help me. *Levite walks over, glances at you, and walks away.*

Levite: I'm in too much of a hurry to stop and help you.

Then God sent a kind person to help me. *Good Samaritan walks over, looks at you, and kneels to help.*

Good Samaritan: I will be glad to help you. *Good Samaritan places bandage on your forehead and helps you hobble to the chair.*

This kind man wasn't even from my own country. He was from Samaria. This Good Samaritan took me to an inn where I could get better. *Good Samaritan pats you on the shoulder.* He freely shared his love and helped me to get well. *Spring to your feet, jubilantly reach toward the sky, and smile.*

Boys and girls, Jesus told this parable to teach us about sharing God's love as good neighbors. Who was the good neighbor in Jesus' story? *Let children respond.* That's right. My neighbor was the Good Samaritan who was not too busy to stop and help me.

Boys and girls, God loves you. He will help you share His love with everyone who needs your help.

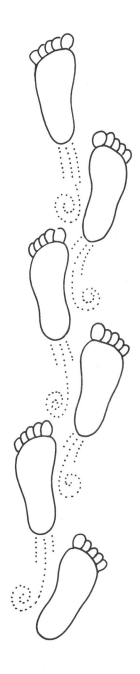

Jesus Heals 10 Sick Men

Scripture: Luke 17:11–19

Central Truth: God loves and cares for us when we are sick and heals our sickness of sin for Jesus' sake.

Props: Cut eye, nose, and mouth holes in 10 paper bags that children will wear over their heads.

Preparation: Quickly rehearse the 11 children who will play the roles of Jesus, the nine sick men, and the tenth man who thanked Jesus. These children stand during the story.

Telling the Story

Boys and girls, today we will learn how Jesus helped 10 sick men who lived long ago. These poor men had a sickness that caused horrible sores on their skin. *Ten children with bags over their heads step forward.*

These sick men were not allowed to live at home with their families. People could not come close to them. No one wanted to get their sickness.

Jesus steps forward. One day the sick men saw Jesus. *The 10 kneel before Jesus.*

Sick men: Jesus, please help us!

Jesus loved those men and wanted to help them.

Jesus *(pointing to the rest of the class):* Go and show yourselves to the priests.

The 10 men did just as Jesus said. As they walked to see the priests, they noticed something wonderful—*(remove paper bags)* their skin was fresh and healthy! Nine of the men hurried to see the priests and go back home. *Nine of the children sit with the rest of the class.* But one man ran back to thank Jesus.

Tenth man *(kneeling before Jesus):* Thank You, Jesus. You made me well!

Jesus: Didn't I make 10 men well? Where are the other nine? Stand up and go. Your faith has made you well. *The tenth child joins the rest of the class.*

Boys and girls, we have a sickness too. It is the sickness of sin. Without Jesus, we would die and have to go to hell. But because Jesus died on the cross to take our punishment, God freely forgives our sin and makes us clean again. We too thank Jesus for taking care of us when we are sick and healing us from the sickness of sin.

Jesus and Zacchaeus

Scripture: Luke 19:1–9

Central Truth: *Jesus forgives your sins and keeps you close to Him.*

Preparation: *Practice reciting the echo pantomime and making the motions. Ask the children to echo your words and mimic your actions.*

Telling the Story

A little man named Zacchaeus
Stretch one hand down toward floor.
Climbed a sycamore tree.
Pretend to climb tree.
Jesus was the one,
Hold up one finger.
He wanted to see.
Cup hand over eyes.

Jesus saw Zacchaeus
Look up.
In the sycamore tree.
Point up.
Jesus said, "Zacchaeus,
Cup hands around mouth and call up into tree.
Come down and eat with Me."
Point to self.

Boys and girls, Zacchaeus wanted to see Jesus so badly that he climbed up in a tree to be able to see Him. Jesus knew that Zacchaeus was lonely and that he had done many things that were wrong. But Jesus loved Zacchaeus and forgave Him.

Jesus keeps us close to Him too. He gave His own life on the cross to pay the price for our sins. He helps us share God's love with other people. One day we will live forever with Him in heaven.

The Widow's Mite

Scripture: Luke 21:1–4

Central Truth: Jesus' gift of life to us on the cross helps us love Him with all we have.

Props: A table, two handfuls of coins plus two pennies, a jar large enough to hold coins, a small paper heart, a magnifying glass

Preparation: Quickly rehearse the three children who will play the roles of two rich people and the poor widow.

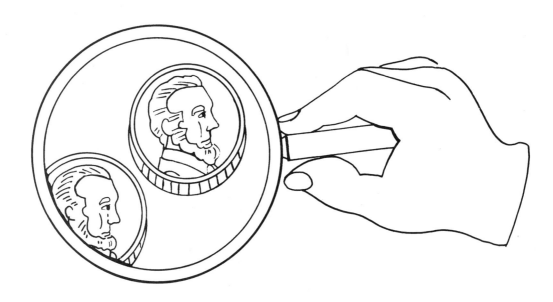

Telling the Story

Hold up coins. One way we can thank God for all the love He gives us is to bring our offering to church. We give our money to help our church do God's work.

Long ago, people brought their offerings to the temple in Jerusalem. One day, Jesus and His disciples watched rich people put their money into the temple treasury.

Rich people *(making a big show of putting handfuls of coins in jar):* We are very rich. We will give a little bit of our money to God. We want everybody to see how much we are giving.

Then a poor widow came along. Her husband had died, and she had no one to take care of her. She could only put two small coins in the offering.

Widow: I love God with all my heart. This is all I have to give. *(Quietly drops two pennies into jar.)* I only wish that I had more money to give to God.

Remove coins from jar and hold them up. Jesus saw the gifts of the rich people who had plenty of money. *Hold up two pennies.* Then He saw the gift of the poor widow who gave all she had.

Ask the children to come to the table. Place the two pennies on the heart and let children take turns looking at them through the magnifying glass. Jesus knew that the widow loved Him with all her heart. She gave all of her money to God, knowing that He would take care of her.

Jesus sees the love in our gifts too, even if they seem small. We think of the great love Jesus gave us in dying on the cross in our place. His love helps us love Him in return.

Jesus Washes His Disciples' Feet

Scripture: John 13:1–17

Central Truth: Jesus loves us with a servant's love, to the point of giving His life for us. His love motivates us to serve others.

Props: Pair of sandals, chair, empty wash basin, empty pitcher, towel

Preparation: Quickly rehearse the 13 children who will play the roles of Jesus and the disciples.

Telling the Story

Boys and girls, today we will learn how Jesus taught His disciples to share His love. Jesus knew that it was almost time to die on the cross for us. He wanted to eat one last meal with His disciples.

In Bible times, people wore sandals *(hold up sandals)* and walked on dusty roads. Their feet got very hot and dirty. When people visited friends in their homes, their friends' servants often washed their feet for them.

As they were eating their last supper together, Jesus got up from the table and *(act out story as you speak)* wrapped a towel around His waist. He poured water into a basin and knelt down to wash the feet of each disciple. First He washed Peter's feet. *Call Peter to sit in chair. Pantomime washing and drying Peter's feet. Then continue with the other disciples.*

Jesus washed the feet of each of His disciples—He even washed Judas' feet, knowing he would betray Him. Washing feet was a lowly job that nobody wanted to do. But Jesus did it gladly, just as He willingly gave His life on the cross for us. His love shows us how to love one another.

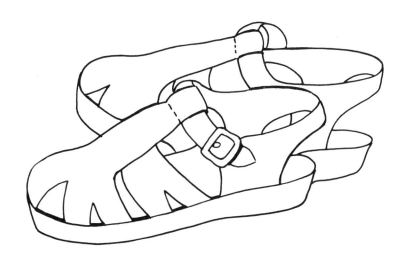

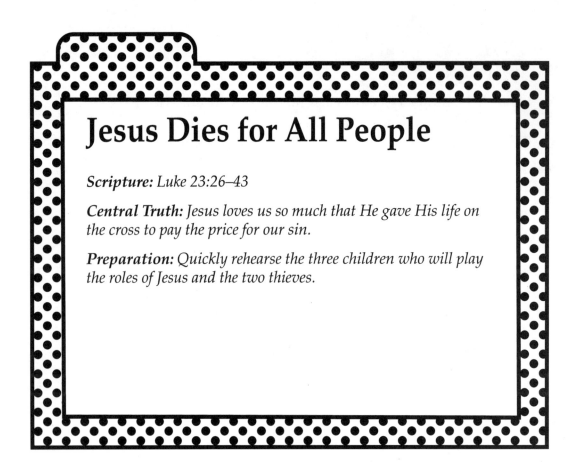

Jesus Dies for All People

Scripture: Luke 23:26–43

Central Truth: Jesus loves us so much that He gave His life on the cross to pay the price for our sin.

Preparation: Quickly rehearse the three children who will play the roles of Jesus and the two thieves.

Telling the Story

Boys and girls, today we will learn how Jesus died on the cross to share His love with all people. Jesus had done nothing wrong. He died on the cross to take the punishment for the wrong things that we have done.

Very early on a Friday morning, soldiers made Jesus walk to a hill outside of Jerusalem. They made a man named Simon walk behind Jesus and carry His heavy wooden cross.

When they came to the hill, the soldiers nailed Jesus to the cross. *Jesus stands with arms outstretched, as if on cross.* The soldiers nailed two other men on crosses, one on Jesus' right and the other on His left. *Two thieves stand with arms outstretched on either side of Jesus.* Both of these men were being punished for doing something wrong. But Jesus had never done anything wrong. He was being punished in our place for our sins.

People started to yell at Jesus and make fun of Him. One of the thieves joined in. He wasn't sorry for what he had done wrong.

Unrepentant thief: If You're the Christ, why don't You get us down from here?

But the man on the other side of Jesus was truly sorry for the wrong that he had done. He believed that Jesus was the Son of God and that He had done nothing wrong.

Repentant thief: Jesus, remember me when You come into Your kingdom.

Jesus: I tell you the truth. Today you will be with Me in heaven.

Boys and girls, Jesus suffered and died on the cross to save us from our sin. What promise did Jesus make to the thief who was sorry? *Let children respond.* Yes, Jesus promised that he would go to heaven with Him.

Jesus loves you so much that He gave His life for you. Now your sins are forgiven and you will get to live with Him in heaven one day.

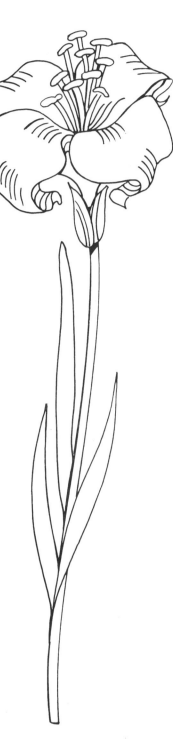

The Resurrection

Scripture: Matthew 28:1–15

Central Truth: Jesus died on the cross and rose again to win us forgiveness of sins and eternal life with Him in heaven.

Preparation: Practice reciting the echo pantomime and making the motions. Ask the children to echo your words and mimic your actions.

Telling the Story

On Easter Sunday,
Smile broadly.
God's angel told
Touch index finger to lips.
Two women named Mary,
Hold up two fingers.
"Jesus rose!
Raise one hand in air.
His tomb is empty."
Make a zero with your fingers.
Jesus lives
Raise one hand in air.
On Easter Sunday!
Smile broadly.

Two women named Mary
Hold up two fingers.
Saw Jesus' tomb.
Cup hand over eyes as if peering into tomb.
His tomb was empty.
Make a zero with your fingers.
Jesus lives
Raise one hand in air.
For you and me!
Point happily to children, then self.

Boys and girls, Jesus did not stay in the grave. He rose again on Easter Sunday. When we die, we will not stay in the grave either. We will wake up and join Jesus in heaven to live with Him forever.

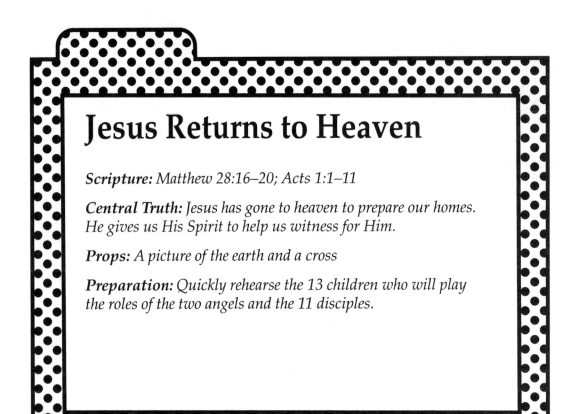

Jesus Returns to Heaven

Scripture: Matthew 28:16–20; Acts 1:1–11

Central Truth: Jesus has gone to heaven to prepare our homes. He gives us His Spirit to help us witness for Him.

Props: A picture of the earth and a cross

Preparation: Quickly rehearse the 13 children who will play the roles of the two angels and the 11 disciples.

Telling the Story

After Jesus rose on Easter, He spent 40 days with His disciples, helping them learn how to share God's love. Then it was time for Him to return to heaven to get our homes ready.

Jesus took His disciples to the top of a hill. There He told them to tell all the people in the world the Good News that they could be saved through believing in Him. Jesus promised to send the Holy Spirit to fill the disciples with the power to share God's love. And Jesus promised that He would always be with them, just as He will always be with us.

Point up. Disciples stare up at the sky. As the disciples watched, Jesus ascended into the sky. He went up and up until the clouds covered Him. The disciples just kept staring up into the sky, wondering where Jesus was, until two angels appeared. *Disciples look at angels in awe.*

Angels: Disciples, why do you stand here, looking into the sky? Jesus has gone to heaven. He will come back again in the same way.

Disciples take heart and smile broadly. Boys and girls, the disciples listened to the two angels. They remembered what Jesus had told them and returned to Jerusalem to wait for a special visit from the Holy Spirit. Soon God's Holy Spirit would fill them with the power to share Jesus' love with people close by and all around the world.

Hold up picture of earth and cross. The disciples knew that Jesus loved them and would return to earth one day to take them to heaven, just as the angels had promised. The disciples spent the rest of their lives sharing the Good News that Jesus died to save us from our sins and then rose again. You can share that Good News too. Jesus promises to help you.

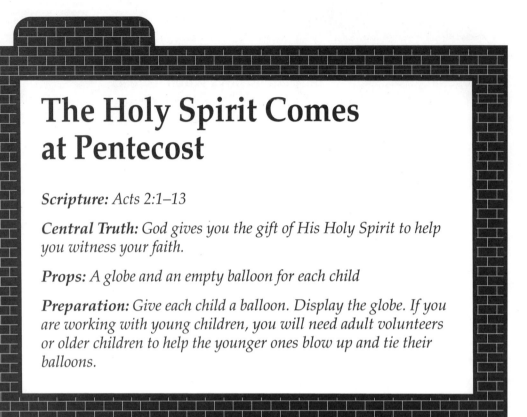

The Holy Spirit Comes at Pentecost

Scripture: *Acts 2:1–13*

Central Truth: *God gives you the gift of His Holy Spirit to help you witness your faith.*

Props: *A globe and an empty balloon for each child*

Preparation: *Give each child a balloon. Display the globe. If you are working with young children, you will need adult volunteers or older children to help the younger ones blow up and tie their balloons.*

Telling the Story

On the day called Pentecost, Jesus' disciples gathered together in a room in Jerusalem. Just 10 days before, the disciples had seen Jesus return to heaven. Jesus had promised that He would send His Holy Spirit to fill them with the power to share His love with all the people of the world. But the disciples still missed Jesus. *Hold up uninflated balloon.* They felt empty without Him.

Suddenly, the disciples heard the sound of a rushing wind. God's Holy Spirit filled them with His power. Let's blow up our empty balloons. *Help children blow up balloons and knot them.*

Now our empty balloons are full and bright. The Holy Spirit came on Pentecost, just as Jesus had promised, and filled the disciples with the power to tell people about God's love.

God sent you His Holy Spirit at your Baptism and filled you with power too. God's Holy Spirit helps you tell your family and your friends that Jesus gave His life on the cross to win you eternal life. Your prayers and offerings help missionaries teach that Good News all around the world.

Let's carry our full, bright balloons around the world and tell everyone about Jesus. *Lead the children in marching around the globe, holding your balloons high. As you march, chant, "Jesus loves you. Jesus died for you and rose again!"*

March back to your seats now, knowing you have the power to share God's love with your family and your friends today.